Contents

What is Buddhism?

Buddhism is based on the teaching of one man in India about 2,500 years ago. He asked, 'Why is there suffering?' and 'How can it be ended?' and eventually he understood. He became known as the Buddha. This means 'the Enlightened One' (the one who has understood the truth).

The Buddha spent the rest of his life teaching people about his ideas, so that they could reach Enlightenment too.

► This statue in Sri Lanka shows the Buddha as peaceful and wise.

The Buddha
and
Buddhism

Ruth Nason

Religious Lives

The Buddha and Buddhism	Krishna and Hinduism
Guru Nanak and Sikhism	Moses and Judaism
Krishna and Hinduism	Muhammad and Islam

For more information on this series and other Wayland titles, go to
www.waylandbooks.co.uk

© White-Thomson Publishing Ltd 2005

Produced for Hodder Wayland by White-Thomson Publishing Ltd
Bridgewater Business Centre, 210 High Street, Lewes, East Sussex BN7 2NH, UK

First published in 2005 by Hodder Wayland, an imprint of Hodder Children's Books
This paperback edition published in 2008 by Wayland, an imprint of Hachette Children's Books

This book is adapted from *The Buddha and Buddhism (Great Religious Leaders series)* by Kerena Marchant,
published by Hodder Wayland in 2002

British Library Cataloguing in Publication Data
Nason, Ruth
The Buddha and Buddhism. - Adapted Ed. (Religious Lives)
1. Gautama Buddha - Juvenile literature 2. Buddhism - Juvenile literature
I. Title II.Marchant, Kerena
294.3'63

ISBN 978 0 7502 4790 0

Printed in China

Wayland
338 Euston Road, London NW1 3BH

Wayland is a division of Hachette Children's Books, an Hachette Livre UK Company
www.hachettelivre.co.uk

Title page: Worshippers at the Shwedagon Pagoda, Rangoon, Burma.

Picture Acknowledgements: The publisher would like to thank the following for permission to reproduce their pictures:
AKG 6 (Jean-Louis Nou), 7 (bottom) (Gilles Mermet), 11 (Gilles Mermet), 12 (Jean-Louis Nou), 17 (Jean-Louis Nou), 31 (Jean-Louis Nou), 42–3 (Erich Lessing), 45 (Gilles Mermet); Art Directors and Trip Photo Library title page (T Bognar), 7 (Dinodia), 8 (H Rogers), 9 (H Rogers), 15 (T Bognar), 21 (top) (P Treanor), 23 (top) (T Bognar), 24 (H Rogers), 35 (C Rennie), 40 (Resource Foto), 45 (bottom) (P Treanor); Britstock-IFA 14 (Bernd Ducke), 18, 23 (bottom) (M Gottschalk), 34 (M Gottschalk), 37 (bottom) (Haga), 44 (Keribar), Chapel Studios/Zul Mukhida cover *top*, 16 (bottom), 19, 22, 27, 29, 36, 37, 41; Circa Photo Library 10, 20 (William Holtby), 25 (MCR), 28, 32 (John Smith), 38 (William Holtby), 39 (William Holtby), Image Bank *cover main*; Impact 16 (top) Mark Henley; Anne & Bury Peerless 26, 33; Tibet Images 4 (Ian Cumming), 5 (Ian Cumming), 21 (bottom) (Ian Cumming), 30 (Neville Hopwood).

Graphics and maps: Tim Mayer.

The Wheel of Life

A demon called Yama holds the 'Wheel of Life'. The wheel is turned by three animals in the centre: a cock for greed, a snake for hatred and a pig for ignorance. This shows the idea that greed, hatred and ignorance keep people in the cycle of rebirth and stop them reaching Enlightenment. In the wheel are pictures of people trying to reach Enlightenment and the Buddha teaching people.

▲ This 'Wheel of Life' illustrates Buddhist beliefs about rebirth and Enlightenment.

What Buddhists believe

Buddhism is different from many other religions. Buddhists do not believe in a God.

Buddhists believe that when someone dies, their soul is reborn into a new life. The way the new life begins is the result of the old life. However, when someone reaches Enlightenment, they become free from the cycle of rebirth.

Another word for the state of Enlightenment is *Nirvana*. Buddhists follow the way of life that the Buddha taught, to try to reach *Nirvana*.

The Life of the Buddha

The Prince

The Buddha was born a prince, called Siddhartha Gautama, near the end of the fifth century BCE. A wise man foretold that Siddhartha would grow up to be great. He said that Siddhartha would either save people from the evils of the world or be a great king.

Siddhartha's father wanted him to become a king. He gave Siddhartha three palaces, and brought him up in happiness and luxury. He stopped Siddhartha from seeing the world outside the palaces.

When Siddhartha grew up, he married Princess Gopa Yasodhara and they had a son. Siddhartha called his son Rahula, which means 'chain'. Siddhartha felt as if he was tied with chains to his luxury life.

At last he decided to see the world beyond the palace and drove out in a chariot.

◀ Prince Siddhartha was born in a garden in Lumbini. His mother, Queen Maya, died a few days later.

Siddhartha saw three examples of suffering: an old man hobbling along, a sick man groaning in pain, and a funeral procession with weeping relatives. He also saw a holy man, who looked happy and peaceful.

Siddhartha wanted to find the truth about why people suffered, and how suffering could be ended. On the night of his 29th birthday he left the palace. In the forest he cut off his hair and changed his rich clothes for rags. Buddhists call this event 'the great Going Forth'.

▲ Outside the palace Siddhartha saw that suffering is a part of life.

Going Forth

The 'great Going Forth' was when Siddhartha left his normal life to seek Enlightenment. Buddhist monks and nuns leave their normal lives in a similar way. Even in their ordinary everyday lives, all Buddhists try to have an attitude of 'going forth'.

► A painting from Thailand shows Siddhartha cutting off his hair.

The Enlightened One

Siddhartha left the palace to seek the truth about how life is. First he tried to learn from famous holy men.

Then he tried to find the truth by living the harsh life of an ascetic. Five people went with him to live in the forest. They ate as little as one grain of rice per day. They whipped themselves and burned their bodies. Sometimes they stood for weeks on end.

After several years Siddhartha was near to death. A woman offered him milk and, as he drank it, he realized that an ascetic's life would not lead him to the truth. His companions were shocked by his change of mind and they left him.

◀ The woman offers milk to Siddhartha.

The bodhi tree at Bodh Gaya

Buddhist pilgrims have always visited the tree where the Buddha meditated. In 1879 the tree withered away, but one branch was transplanted and a new tree grew from it.

► The Buddha meditates under the *bodhi* tree at Bodh Gaya.

On his 35th birthday Siddhartha arrived at Bodh Gaya. He made a grass mat, placed it under a tree and sat, determined to find the truth. He began to meditate.

On the first night of meditation he saw all his past lives and lived through all his experiences again. On the second night he saw all other beings go through the cycle of birth and rebirth. On the third night he reached Enlightenment, understanding clearly the way things are. As he became Enlightened, he became free from suffering. His cycle of rebirth was over.

The Preacher

After the Buddha reached Enlightenment, he wanted to help all beings reach Enlightenment too. For the next 45 years he travelled around India teaching the *Dharma,* the way to Enlightenment.

First he went to find his five companions from the forest. They would not believe that he had become Enlightened, but eventually his calm face persuaded them to listen to him. He preached his first sermon to them, at Sarnath, and at the end they all decided to follow the *Dharma*.

The Buddha and his five companions attracted many followers and soon 70 monks followed the Buddha on his journeys. Many people, including kings, also became Buddhists.

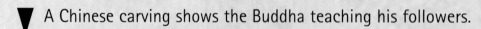

▼ A Chinese carving shows the Buddha teaching his followers.

This painting in Thailand shows the Buddha with his father's courtiers at the palace.

After some years, the Buddha arrived at his father's palace in Kapilavastu. His father and all his courtiers became Buddhists. The Buddha's son became a monk.

Buddhist monks and ordinary Buddhists formed a community called the *sangha*. The monks preached the *Dharma* and the laity (the ordinary Buddhists) provided food and shelter for the monks and built monasteries, or *viharas*, for them.

Kisagotami's story

When Kisagotami's child died, she wanted the Buddha to bring him back to life. The Buddha told her to bring him a mustard seed from a house where nobody had died. She went to many houses but could not find any house where nobody had died. She realized the Buddha had taught her a truth about life and wanted to learn more from him. She became a Buddhist nun.

The Death of the Buddha

The Buddha wanted the *sangha* to carry on after his death. He wanted people to go on teaching the *Dharma* so that others could find the way to Enlightenment.

Near the end of his life, aged 80, the Buddha set out to visit his monks for the last time. He was weak and on the way he ate bad food and became ill. Yet he was determined to travel on and arrived at Kusinagara. The monks and many noblemen and kings were waiting for him in the wood outside the town. They were sad, knowing that their leader was dying.

▼ This cave painting in Sri Lanka shows the Buddha waiting for his death. Around him monks and princes wait and pray.

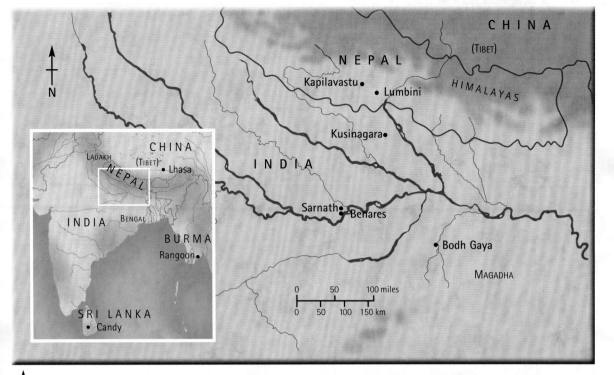

▲ The places where the Buddha lived are in India and present-day Nepal. Later his teaching spread to Sri Lanka, China, Burma and other Asian countries.

The Buddha bathed in the river and put on his best clothes to preach his last sermon. He went over all the main points of his teaching, then said, 'I am about to leave you. If you have any doubts about the *Dharma*, ask me now, so that argument will not divide you later.' The monks promised that they had no doubts.

The Buddha blessed everybody, lay down on a couch with his head facing north and died peacefully. The monks and kings wept. Many accounts say that it became dark, the earth trembled and the trees shed their leaves.

Buddhists believe that when he died, the Buddha entered the state of 'final *Nirvana*'. They celebrate the passing of the Buddha as Parinirvana Day.

The Buddha's Teachings

The Middle Way

The Buddha's teaching is called the *Dharma*, which means 'Truth' and 'a way of life'. The Buddha taught people a way of life which can lead to Enlightenment. He called it 'the Middle Way'.

▲ Buddhist monks wear simple robes. These monks in Tibet are sharing their daily meal under the shade of some trees.

The Buddha himself experienced a life of great luxury at the palace and a life of great hardship as an ascetic (see page 8). These were extreme ways of life and neither led to Enlightenment. The Buddha reached Enlightenment when he followed a simple lifestyle, in between the two extremes.

Therefore he taught people to follow a simple lifestyle. For example, Buddhists do not feast or fast at festivals. They share a simple community meal. They do not dress in expensive, showy clothes, but try to wear simple, practical clothes.

The Buddha explained that this Middle Way is like:

> *A lamp for those who are in darkness*
>
> *A mother for children*
>
> *A ferry for those who need a boat*
>
> *A fire to warm those who are cold*
>
> *A garment for those who are naked.*

The two extremes

There are two extremes that should not be practised: that devoted to passions and luxury ... and that devoted to self-mortification ...

Dharmapada

► A Buddhist family shares their food with some nuns. This will be the nuns' meal for the day.

The Four Noble Truths

The Buddha taught that the Middle Way is based on Four Noble Truths. They are:

1 All life is suffering

Happiness never lasts and suffering comes to everyone. Prince Siddhartha realized this when he went outside the palace and saw an old man, a sick man in pain, and people mourning the death of a loved one.

This *bodhi* tree has grown from a branch of the tree where the Buddha meditated and reached Enlightenment (see page 9).

An elderly woman makes an offering to the Buddha.

2 The cause of suffering is craving

Craving means always wanting something. Craving causes ignorance, greed and hatred – the forces which turn the Wheel of Life (see page 5). This keeps people in the cycle of rebirth and away from Enlightenment.

3 There can be release from craving

Release from craving can come if a person gives up their selfish wants. To give up craving, they need to understand that it causes suffering.

4 The way to release is to follow the Noble Eightfold Path

The Buddha taught people eight ways of living to become free from craving. These eight ways make up the Noble Eightfold Path (see pages 18-20), which is the same as the Middle Way.

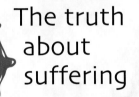 In some countries children become monks and nuns. They learn to follow the Noble Eightfold Path.

The truth about suffering

This, O monk, is the noble truth of suffering: death is suffering; the presence of objects we hate is suffering; separation from objects we love is suffering; not to obtain what we desire is suffering. Clinging to life is suffering. Existence is suffering.

Vinaya Pitaka

The Noble Eightfold Path

The Buddha taught people a way of life which would help them to overcome greed and hatred and develop love and contentment. He divided this way of life into eight parts, but they make one whole, like a wheel with eight spokes. He said that people should try to follow all eight parts of the Path. They are:

1 Right understanding of the Four Noble Truths

Buddhists must first understand the Four Noble Truths. Unless they do, they cannot understand themselves, others and the universe in which they live.

2 Right thoughts

A Buddhist must think only good, kind thoughts.

▼ A monk in Thailand prays in front of the feet of a huge statue of the Buddha.

3 Right speech

Everything Buddhists say must be thoughtful, truthful and kind.

4 Right action

Buddhists must be kind to others and towards all living creatures. This leads many Buddhists to be vegetarian, so that no living creature is killed to provide their food. Many Buddhists follow the path of 'Right action' by doing things to care for the environment.

▲ A woman offers flowers at a Buddhist shrine in Sri Lanka. She tries to follow the way of life that the Buddha taught.

5 Right livelihood

Livelihood means the work a person does to earn their living. Buddhists must choose work which allows them to practise 'Right action'. Many Buddhists say it is not possible for a Buddhist to be a soldier and to kill people. Many Buddhists would not work as meat-farmers, fishermen or butchers, as those jobs involve killing animals.

▼ Buddhists like these nuns say that following the Noble Eightfold Path gives them a sense of peace.

6 Right effort

The sixth part of the Noble Eightfold Path is that Buddhists must always try hard to banish hatred, greed and ignorance and to develop kindness, generosity and wisdom.

7 Right mindfulness

Buddhists must try always to be aware of themselves and of others. To do this, they must stay calm and act in a careful way.

8 Right concentration or right meditation

Meditation is the practice of clearing one's mind and, in the calm, concentrating on one thing. Buddhists believe that 'Right meditation' is a way to Enlightenment, as it was for the Buddha (see page 9).

▲ Pictures and statues of the Buddha help this
monk to focus his mind as he meditates.

The Wheel of the Dharma

The Noble Eightfold Path is often represented as an eight-spoked wheel. Each spoke represents one part of the Eightfold Path. The middle, where the spokes meet, stands for *Nirvana*. The wheel is a complete circle. This shows that the Buddha's teaching covers all aspects of life.

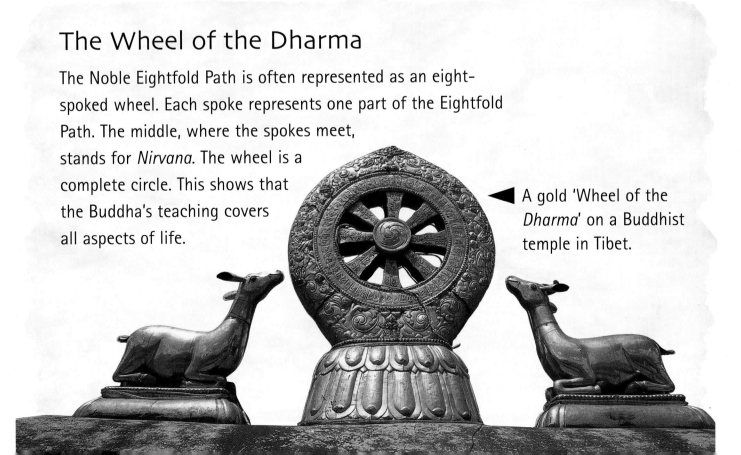

◀ A gold 'Wheel of the *Dharma*' on a Buddhist temple in Tibet.

The sangha

The Buddha realized that it would be easier for people to follow the Noble Eightfold Path if they joined together as a Buddhist community. People in the community could support each other. The Buddha set up a community called the *sangha* and gave rules for its members to follow. The *sangha* included monks, nuns and lay Buddhists.

▼ Lay Buddhists in Sri Lanka give the monks the everyday things they need, such as food, new robes, pots and writing paper.

The Five Precepts

The Five Precepts are rules for everyone in the *sangha*. They say that Buddhists must abstain from: harming others, stealing, sexual misconduct, false speech, and alcohol and drugs.

The life of lay Buddhists

The Buddha told lay Buddhists to look after their parents, respect their elders and support the monks and nuns by giving them food and robes.

He said that lay people as well as monks could reach Enlightenment.

The life of monks and nuns

The Buddha believed that the best way to follow the Eightfold Path and reach Enlightenment was to become a monk or nun. He gave many special rules for monks and nuns to follow.

Monks and nuns must spend their time meditating, studying and teaching. To leave them free to concentrate on this, the Buddha told the lay Buddhists to provide the monks and nuns with their daily meal.

▲ Lay Buddhists pray and meditate at a temple in Burma.

▼ Buddhist monks in India and South-east Asia wear saffron-coloured robes, as the Buddha did.

The Three Refuges

When someone becomes a Buddhist, they say:

I go to the Buddha for refuge.

I go to the Dharma for refuge.

I go to the Sangha for refuge.

Meditation

Meditation is an important part of following the Buddhist way of life (see page 20). The Buddha reached Enlightenment through meditating. There are also legends about the Buddha meditating when he was a boy in his palaces.

Like other people who practise meditation, Buddhists say that they must concentrate to clear their mind. To do this, they need to be positive and feel at peace. These feelings come from following the Noble Eightfold Path. It's also important to sit comfortably. Being uncomfortable makes it hard to concentrate on clearing the mind.

Some Buddhists say that when their head is free of thoughts and worries about everyday existence, then they feel a sense of 'inner freedom' and this is meditation.

▼ These Buddhists meditating in England sit in the position they find most comfortable.

A Tibetan Buddhist shrine

Tibetan Buddhists usually meditate in front of a shrine. On it they place:

- two pots of water to honour the Buddha, one to wash his feet and one for him to drink;
- flowers;
- incense;
- perfume;
- a light;
- food;
- a shell.

On this Tibetan Buddhist shrine there are prayer ribbons (left) as well as the eight objects mentioned above.

Buddhists sometimes meditate together and sometimes meditate alone. To help them meditate, some focus on an object, a flower, an image of the Buddha or on their breathing.

Japanese Zen Buddhists focus on a riddle to help the mind break free.

The Sacred Texts

The Buddha taught people through sermons, stories and riddles and by giving them tasks to try and rules to follow. He did not write anything down. His attendant, Ananda, remembered all his teachings and could recite them later for other people to hear.

▲ The Buddha preaches his first sermon at Sarnath.

The Pali Canon

At a meeting after the Buddha's death his followers reported all the teachings he had given them. The senior monks listened and agreed on a version that could be learned by heart and passed on.

For hundreds of years the teachings were passed on in this way. Then, in the first century BCE, they were written down in the Pali language. These writings are called the Pali Canon.

This happened in the country that we now call Sri Lanka. Monks and merchants travelled from there to other countries, taking the Pali Canon with them, and Buddhism spread through the eastern world.

People thought that the Buddha's teachings, passed from generation to generation, were like the baskets of materials that are passed along a line of builders. The Pali Canon was in three sections and so it was called the *Tripitaka* (three baskets).

Today it has been translated into many languages. Many Buddhists learn Pali in order to read it in its original form.

Other scriptures

As Buddhism spread, other scriptures were written, for example in Chinese, Japanese and Tibetan. These scriptures took in local traditions and different ideas about the Buddha's teachings.

▼ The scriptures of the Pali Canon were first written on strips of palm leaves.

The Pali language

Pali is an ancient language used in Sri Lanka and some areas of India. It was used in Magadha in India (near present-day Bengal), where the monks decided how to pass on the Buddha's teachings. Pali is thought to be a dialect of Sanskrit, India's oldest language.

The Vinaya Pitaka

This first section of the Pali Canon is known as the 'basket of rules' for monks and nuns. It contains 227 rules for monks and more rules for nuns.

◀ The scriptures were written in ink on dried palm leaves. These were tied together to make a book.

The Sutra Pitaka

This is the second section of the Pali Canon. It is often called the 'basket of discourses' (talks). One part of it is the *Dharmapada*, giving the Buddha's teaching about the Four Noble Truths and the Noble Eightfold Path. This is written in beautiful Pali verse. Some Buddhists learn its 423 verses by heart.

The Abhidharma Pitaka

This third section of the Pali Canon is the 'basket of philosophical teaching'. It develops the teachings in the *Sutra Pitaka*.

The teachings of other Buddhists

As well as books giving the Buddha's teaching, there are many books of teachings from other people who reached Enlightenment by following the Buddha's way. A famous one is the *Vimalakirti Sutra*. Vimalakirti was a lay Buddhist who showed many signs of reaching Enlightenment.

▲ Ancient copies of the Buddhist scriptures are kept at Buddhist monasteries. Monks also continue the art of writing the scriptures on palm leaves.

The Tibetan Book of the Dead

This book is read to someone who has died to guide them between death and the next rebirth. If they follow its advice, they could reach Enlightenment and not be reborn.

Tibetan Buddhists believe that many scriptures were hidden until the *sangha* was ready to understand them. Many of these hidden scriptures, including the *Tibetan Book of the Dead*, have been found since Buddhism started. Others are still being found.

The Sacred Places

Before he died, the Buddha named four places where pilgrims should go to remember his teachings: Lumbini, his birthplace; Bodh Gaya, where he found Enlightenment; Sarnath, where he preached his first sermon; and Kusinagara, where he died.

In Ladakh, north India, people have no transport. It takes several days to reach their nearest Buddhist monastery.

However, when the Buddha died, his followers argued over where to bury him. A wise monk suggested dividing the Buddha's remains and burying them in several places. This led to more places of pilgrimage.

Stupas

The Buddha's remains were buried in ten dome-shaped mounds called *stupas*. There is much debate today about their actual sites.

As Buddhism spread, the Buddha's remains were divided again to create new *stupas*. The *stupas* also became more lavish. It is said that a tooth of the Buddha was taken from the *stupa* at Sarnath to Candy in Sri Lanka when Buddhism spread there. King Ashoka, an Indian Buddhist king, is said to have built 84,000 stupas! Most are said to house a relic of the Buddha.

Wherever Buddhism spread, people wanted places to visit as pilgrims. *Stupas* were built not just for the remains of the Buddha, but also for the remains of other Buddhists who had reached Enlightenment. Some *stupas* were built to contain sacred texts.

The Temple of the Countless Buddhas

At Borobudur in Java there is a huge *stupa* on top of a hill. To reach it, pilgrims pass hundreds of other *stupas*, each with a statue of the Buddha. The pilgrims stop and kiss the hands and feet of these statues. The 5-km journey to the main *stupa* is said to symbolize the journey of a soul towards *Nirvana* or Enlightenment.

▼ Many Buddhists believe that remains of the Buddha are buried in the hill under the main *stupa* at Borobudur.

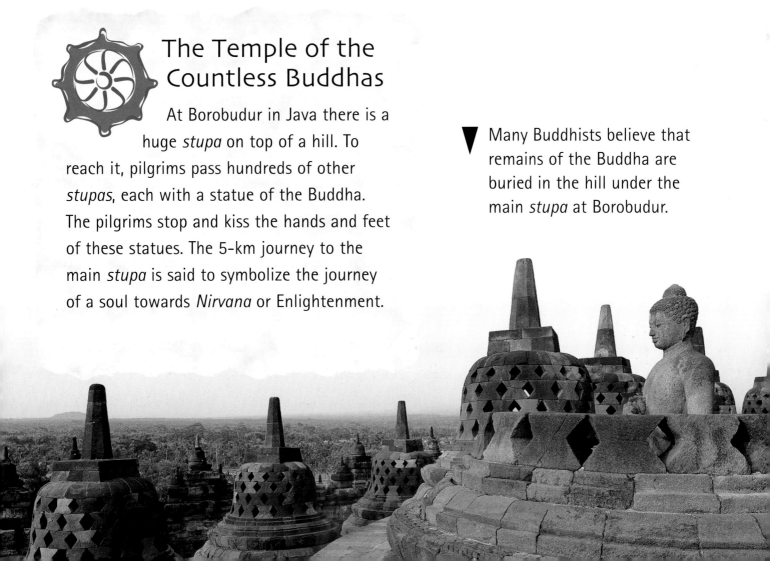

Sarnath

In the Buddha's time Sarnath was a peaceful wood, where people went to live to seek the truth. The Buddha preached his first sermon there and after his death Sarnath became the most important Buddhist centre in India. One of the first *stupas* and a large monastery were built there. Only ruins remain today. Pilgrims visit to meditate and pray.

▼ Today the ruins at Sarnath are part of a peaceful deer park.

Lumbini and Kapilavastu

The Buddha's birthplace in a garden at Lumbini and the site of his father's palace in Kapilavastu are in present-day Nepal. Both sites were destroyed hundreds of years ago by Muslim invaders.

At Lumbini, pilgrims can visit the pool where Queen Maya bathed before giving birth to

Siddhartha. They can see the tree that sheltered her and her baby.

Not far away are the remains of a huge pillar built by the great King Ashoka. He visited Lumbini as a pilgrim in the second century.

Also nearby, archaeologists have discovered the remains of a palace with moats and gates. It is believed to be the palace at Kapilavastu.

The government of Nepal plans to develop both this site and Lumbini into major tourist centres.

The place at which the devoted person can say: 'Here the wheel of the Dharma was set in motion by the Buddha!' is a place to visit with feelings of reverence.

Mahaparinirvana Sutra

▼ In the foreground is the pool in Lumbini where Queen Maya bathed. In the distance is King Ashoka's pillar.

The Shwedagon Pagoda of Burma

Buddhism spread to Burma in South-east Asia and became the major religion there. The Shwedagon Pagoda in Burma's capital, Rangoon, is one of the most impressive Buddhist temples in the world. It houses many shrines and *stupas*. The main *stupa* is made entirely of gold and precious stones.

Pagoda is another word for a *stupa*. The Shwedagon Pagoda is said to house eight sacred hairs of the Buddha. Buddhist pilgrims visit the Pagoda from all over Burma and the world.

◀ Outside the main *stupa* of the Shwedagon Pagoda is a shrine with a statue of the Buddha.

The Ryoanji Temple of Japan

In Japan a type of Buddhism developed called Zen Buddhism. Zen Buddhists place great importance on clearing the mind of all distractions so it can be completely calm for meditation.

The Ryoanji Temple is a Zen Buddhist temple. The temple building is a simple wooden one and its garden is made only of stone and gravel with a few mossy rocks. Zen monks tend the garden, patiently raking the gravel to help them meditate. Visiting the garden helps pilgrims to feel calm too.

Tea and Zen meditation

Sometimes the monks at the Ryoanji Temple offer visitors tea. Zen monks follow a simple, formal way of brewing and drinking tea to help them meditate.

◀ Looking at the carefully raked stones in the Ryoanji Temple garden helps visitors to meditate.

Festivals

In different countries Buddhists celebrate different festivals. However, many of these festivals celebrate the birth, the Enlightenment and the death of the Buddha.

Wesak

These three events are celebrated at the festival of Wesak in India, Sri Lanka and countries in South-east Asia such as Thailand and Burma.

In Thailand and Burma, the festival focuses most on the Buddha's Enlightenment. Lights are lit as a symbol of Enlightenment. In Thailand caged birds are set free as a symbol of the freedom from suffering that Enlightenment brings.

In most places at Wesak the scriptures are taken out from the *viharas* and their pages are dusted.

▲ At Wesak in Sri Lanka people make lit-up pictures of events in the Buddha's life.

Monks and lay people walk three times around their *vihara*, temple or pagoda. As they walk they think about the Buddha, the *Dharma* and the *sangha*.

► Children give their parents presents for Wesak.

Hana Matsuri and Parinirvana Day

The Hana Matsuri festival takes place in April in Japan. It is a flower festival and celebrates the birth of the Buddha. Places are decorated with flowers to represent the garden where the Buddha was born.

A white elephant is part of the legend about the Buddha's birth and so a model of a white elephant is placed in the courtyard of monasteries. There are food stalls, dancing and acrobatics.

Buddhists in Japan mark the death of the Buddha on Parinirvana Day in February. They turn off the lights and meditate in darkness for some time.

▼ Children in Japan take part in a procession for Hana Matsuri.

The Rains Retreat

Monsoon winds cause countries in Asia to have a rainy season and a dry season. The Buddha and his monks retreated to the *vihara* in the rainy season. They could not travel, as many areas became flooded and the roads were muddy. The monks used the time to meditate, study and think about their religion.

Today monks and nuns in Sri Lanka, Thailand, Burma and India have 'Rains Retreat' festivals. The rainy season can last as long as three months and the monks and nuns use this time to read the scriptures, pray and meditate together. Some children and young adults become temporary monks and nuns for the period.

In Thailand the Rains Retreat begins with a huge procession of floats. On them are giant candles which burn throughout the three months.

▼ During the Rains Retreat some people spend several days at a monastery to meditate and study Buddhist teachings.

Just before the rains end, the monks or nuns meet and confess and ask forgiveness for any wrong acts. Then the Rains Retreat ends with a festival called Kathina.

Kathina

At Kathina, lay Buddhists go to the *vihara* with gifts for the monks. Traditional gifts are new robes.

Often one robe is offered to the monks in a special ceremony. For example, in Thailand there are boat races and then the king presents the robe. After this, candles are lit and floated on the water. The candles are made to look like Buddhist temples.

▼ A monk receives a new robe, woven by lay Buddhists. The white cloth will be dyed saffron-coloured in a special ceremony.

The Festival of the Tooth

Many Buddhist festivals took over festivals that were already celebrated in a country before it became Buddhist.

In Sri Lanka, before Buddhism arrived, there was a festival in which a pole was carried on the back of a grey elephant. The pole was a symbol of power, which passed through the king to the people.

In the fourth century King Megavanna became a Buddhist and made Sri Lanka a Buddhist country. He ordered that, instead of the pole, the Buddha's sacred tooth should be carried on the elephant's back. This has grown into the two-week Festival of the Tooth.

▼ Buddhists and Hindus throw flowers in front of the elephants at the Festival of the Tooth.

The Buddha's Tooth?

The relic that is said to be the Buddha's tooth is kept inside seven caskets. The keys to the caskets are divided among four people. All four must be present to open the caskets. People who have seen the tooth report it to be 7.5 cm long, not looking like a human tooth at all!

Two elephant tusks are displayed in front of the chamber where the 'sacred tooth' is kept at the Temple in Candy.

For the festival the Buddha's tooth is taken from the Temple of the Tooth in Candy and carried through the town in a procession of richly dressed elephants. The elephant carrying the tooth is called 'the tusker' and is dressed in embroidered cloth lined with tiny light bulbs.

Images of Hindu gods are also part of the procession and Hindus join Buddhists to celebrate the festival. In Sri Lanka today Buddhists and Hindus are divided, but this festival unites them in a way that politics cannot.

Guru Rinpoche's Birthday

As well as festivals to celebrate events in the Buddha's life, there are festivals to remember other Buddhists who became great teachers.

Guru Rinpoche was the founder of Tibetan Buddhism. His teachings were mostly about meditation. Therefore meditation is the main way in which his birthday is celebrated.

Tibetan Buddhists go to the monastery to pray, chant and meditate with the monks. First they go to the monastery's shrine room and make offerings of food, water and light.

▼ Pictures like this help Tibetan Buddhists to visualize Guru Rinpoche when they meditate.

Then the chanting begins, and becomes more and more powerful. The chanting helps to clear people's minds and they enter a state of meditation.

Tibetan Buddhists believe that this state of meditation helps them to be wise and kind and to follow the way of life that the Buddha taught. Guru Rinpoche said that, to meditate well, people should see a picture in their mind, for example of the Buddha. At this festival people try to visualize Guru Rinpoche. Afterwards everyone at the monastery eats a meal together, sharing the food that has been offered.

Guru Rinpoche

Guru Rinpoche travelled from India, over the Himalayas, to take Buddhism to Tibet. Many others had died on this dangerous journey, frozen to death or killed by animals or bandits.

His name was Padma Sambhava, but the Tibetans named him Guru Rinpoche, which means 'precious teacher'. He converted many Tibetans to Buddhism.

Buddhism Today

Today there are 400 to 500 million Buddhists.
Most live in Asia.

The monks who took Buddhism to other countries would have dressed like this monk of today.

Buddhism in India

Buddhism became popular in north India, where the Buddha had lived. In the second century CE, an Indian king called Ashoka became a Buddhist. He set up a Buddhist kingdom, with laws based on the Buddha's teaching.

After Ashoka died, Buddhism began to decline in India. Most Indians were Hindus. In the ninth century Muslims began to invade India and Buddhist temples and shrines were destroyed.

The spread of Buddhism

King Ashoka sent Buddhists to spread the religion to Sri Lanka. It became the main centre of Buddhism and the Pali Canon (see page 26) was written there.

Buddhism then spread south-east, to modern-day Vietnam, Thailand and Burma. Monks and traders travelling north-east took Buddhism to Tibet, China and Japan.

Buddhism under threat

In the twentieth century China, Tibet and Vietnam came under communist rule. Communists forbid people to practise any religion. However, some Buddhist monks and nuns have made peaceful protests against the communists. The monks and nuns are persecuted in these countries. Many have fled.

Buddhism in the West

Also in the twentieth century Buddhism spread to the USA and Europe. Some people in the West turn away from religion because, in the modern world, they do not believe in God. Buddhism does not involve belief in a god, and the Buddha's teaching about how to live good lives seems very relevant in the modern, materialistic world.

▲ A Tibetan Buddhist nun prays, holding a photo of the Dalai Lama, the Tibetan Buddhist leader. Monks and nuns in Tibet keep their faith in spite of persecution.

► Many people from the West visit countries such as India, Sri Lanka and Thailand, to learn more about Buddhism.

Glossary

ascetic   someone who chooses to follow a very strict, harsh lifestyle, often for religious reasons.

BCE   Before the Common Era. This is used in dates instead of BC (Before Christ), especially when talking about religions other than Christianity. See also CE.

bodhi tree   a type of tree under which the Buddha meditated and reached Enlightenment.

canon   a group of sacred books.

CE   In the Common Era. This is used in dates instead of AD (*Anno Domini*) when talking about religions other than Christianity.

ceremony   a set way of celebrating an event.

chant   to half-speak and half-sing words, without musical accompaniment.

confess   to admit one's wrongdoings.

Dharma   the Buddha's teaching about the way things are and the way people should live.

Enlightenment   a state of understanding the truth about the way life is, and becoming free from the cycle of rebirth.

holy men   in India, men who devote their whole lives to praying and meditating.

incense   material that is burned or heated to release a perfume, used in religious ceremonies.

laity   the people who belong to a religion but are not priests, monks or nuns.

lay Buddhist   a Buddhist who is not a monk or a nun.

monastery   a place where monks live, meditate and study.

monk   a man who devotes his life to meditation, study and teaching about the *Dharma*. Monks take vows to follow a simple lifestyle, depending on the laity for all they need.

Nirvana   another word for the state of Enlightenment.

nun   the female equivalent of a monk.

offering   a gift made as part of worship.

pagoda   a word used in some countries for a *stupa*.

pilgrims   people who travel to a holy place for religious reasons.

preach   to talk to people about religion.

relic   part of a dead holy person's body, or an object that belonged to them.

saffron   an orange-yellow colour.

sangha   the whole Buddhist community of monks, nuns and lay Buddhists.

sermon   a talk on a religious subject.

shrine   a holy place, sometimes containing a religious statue.

soul   the spiritual part of a person which some people believe lives on after death.

stupa   a burial mound or a building housing a relic of the Buddha or another sacred object.

temple   a building for worship.

vihara   a Buddhist word for a monastery.

Further Information

Books

21st Century Religions: Buddhism
by Anita Ganeri (Wayland, 2005)

A Year of Religious Festivals: My Buddhist Year
by Cath Senker (Wayland, 2003)

Bodh Gaya by Mandy Ross (Heinemann Library, 2002)

Buddhism (Eyewitness Guide) by Philip Wilkinson and Peggy Morgan (Dorling Kindersley, 2003)

Buddhist Vihara (Keystones series) by Anita Ganeri (A. and C. Black, 2000)

Facts About Buddhism by Alison Cooper (Wayland, 2004)

I Belong To the Buddhist Faith by Katie Dicker and Nisansa de Silva (Wayland, 2008)

Religions of the World: The Buddhist World By Anne Bancroft (Wayland, 2001)

Sacred Texts: The Tipitaka and Buddhism by Anita Ganeri (Evans Publishing Group, 2003)

Storyteller: Buddhist Stories by Antia Ganeri (Evans Publishing Group, 2000)

The Barefoot Book of Buddhist Tales, edited by Sherab Chodzin et. al. (Barefoot Books, 1999)

World Religions Today: Buddhism by Karen Walker (Wayland, 2007)

Resources for teachers

http://www.reonline.org.uk
A 'family of websites' including some for teachers and some for pupils. Serves as a gateway to over 300 RE resources drawn from all over the web.

http://www.theredirectory.org.uk

http://www.clear-vision.org
Website of the Clear Vision Trust, a UK charity associated with the Friends of the Western Buddhist Order. Offers educational resources (including DVDs, artefacts and posters) and teacher training.

BBC Education produces schools media resources on different faiths. See:
http://www.bbc.co.uk/schools

Channel 4 produces schools media resources on different faiths, including *Animated World Faiths*. Download catalogue from:
http://www.channel4.com/learning

The Institute for Indian Art and Culture
The Bhavan Centre, 4a Castletown Road, West Kensington, London W14 9HQ
Tel: 0207 381 3086   http://www.bhavan.net

Index